A P.

Devotional Readings for Mothers

by

JEANETTE LOCKERBIE

MOODY PRESS

CHICAGO

© 1971 by
THE MOODY BIBLE INSTITUTE
OF CHICAGO

ISBN: 0-8024-6625-7

Twelfth Printing, 1980

Printed in the United States of America

Foreword

As a psychologist, in my years of working with families, I have come to the strong conviction that nothing is more important for emotional well-being than the early relationships between the child and his mother.

In writing a foreword to this new book by Jeannette Lockerbie, I can say unhesitatingly that mothers will receive insight and practical help from these pages. Mrs. Lockerbie is not only a gifted writer but she has the wisdom that comes from a sound knowledge of the Word of God. As editor of *Psychology for Living,* she works closely with our staff of Christian psychologists and is uniquely equipped to write from both the scriptural and the psychological point of view.

Her own children—her son, an outstanding Christian educator and writer; her daughter, a missionary nurse and writer—are, however, the best endorsement of her qualifications to speak to other mothers. I pray—and predict—that *A Plate of Hot Toast* will be wonderfully used of God.

Dr. Clyde M. Narramore

1

A Plate of Hot Toast

I would like to pay tribute to my own mother. Almost certainly, the words *child psychology* were not part of her well-rounded vocabulary. Nevertheless, her very special thoughtfulnesses engraved on my childhood, etchings which are as clear today as when I skipped home from school in those long ago days in my native Scotland.

A fire glowed in the big kitchen fireplace; and on a swinging hob, a plate of hot, buttery toast greeted me as I tossed my schoolbooks down.

Just bread toasted to a golden brown? No, much more than that. A mother who was home and watched for her children as one by one we rounded the corner to our street; a mother to whom we could pour out immediately, while they were fresh in our minds, the events of our usually uneventful day. And she listened.

My mother had time to teach us to sing. She sang with us until we knew all the beautiful old ballads of our country. She sang the old hymns so that, although

5

I did not know the Saviour until years later, I had this golden store she had given me. It's with me still.

Contrast the poor children in many a home today. Poor, though they may possess every up-to-the-minute gadget of electronics and cosmetics. Poor, because their mother is not home.

Consider the child who dawdles her way home. Why hurry? One second grader seated on the curb near her home, petting a stray kitten, voiced it all when she explained to a concerned teenage neighbor, "Nobody's home at my house and the kitty loves me."

If this little article seems to come through to you as a plea to be "a mommy who's home," you read it right.

There will be time for many things as you move on from being the mother of little children, but there will never again be time to do things for and with these little children. One of the most telling statements I have heard lately came from the lips of Dr. Clyde Narramore: "Sadly, the film of childhood cannot be rewound for a second run."

The kind of memories that warm my heart now, and which I suppose I took for granted at the time, cost my mother plenty. Good memories do cost—in time, in unselfishness, in understanding. But they last when all the things we can give a child are discarded, perhaps relegated to the garbage.

Think of your delight in later years when your son or daughter recalls, "Mom, it was just great coming home from school. *You* were there." One grown-up daughter

6

reminded her mother, "I loved to look through the front window and see you ironing."

Ironing or warm toast, they spell the same: "Mom's home."

2

The Now People

Have you listened to a group of mothers as they voiced their dreams of tomorrow? Did the rosy future sometimes come through like this?

"When the twins are off my hands—"

"I can hardly wait until Billy goes to kindergarten—"

"Think of all the time I'll have when the kids are in school and out of my way!"

A sensitive child can be hurt by hearing such talk, however lightly the words are spoken. Cindy, playing with the neighbor children and within earshot of the mothers, overheard the remark, "When Cindy's out of my way all day—"

Half an hour later, when the mothers gathered their broods before going home to prepare dinner, Cindy could not be found.

"She was playing with us," a playmate assured Cindy's mother.

A search of the play area proved futile, and the frantic mother began to be haunted by dread fears for her little girl. Fortunately, Cindy's little feet had not carried her far, and within the hour her mother was eagerly gathering her into her arms.

"Why did you leave the other children? Where were you going?"

"Mamma," the child whimpered, "I heard you talking, and I thought you wanted me to go away."

We can all imagine ourselves in this mother's place at that moment. To be sure, it's an extreme case. But it happened. A child put her own construction on what had been said by her mother—a mother who was dreaming aloud about a faraway tomorrow.

This example may make us appreciate today. While we should make provision for the tomorrow that possibly will bring some leisure time and less regimentation of our schedule, we should never be caught moaning that our home, our children, or our husband is cramping our style.

"Sufficient unto the day is the evil [and the good] thereof" (Mt 6:34).

The now people enjoy God's gifts while it is today. And their children are aware of this.

3

"Hopeth All Things"

Do we really expect the best of our kids in school work, cooperation in the home, sports achievements, and life attitudes?

Mary Glenn was stopped short one afternoon as she passed the room of her teenage son Carl. She heard, "I might as well do it. I'll get blamed anyway. You know Mom."

She couldn't find out what was being discussed by her two boys without revealing that she had heard part of the conversation. But the awful truth shook her considerably. Could Carl possibly be right? Was she indeed guilty of this kind of suspicious attitude? She was reminded, in the midst of her disturbing thoughts, of something she had once read: "Suspicion creates that which it suspects."

From that day on, this mother was more careful. No more sharp-tongued "You're late—as usual," or "I suppose you left your room in a mess," or "Listening to records, and your homework isn't even half done!"

A new "hopeth all things" spirit replaced the negative prejudging, and the change was reflected in both sons in this home. A new frankness sprang up between the boys and their parents as their mother made them aware of her trust and expectation.

Can we doubt this is one of the factors of love? Love "beareth all things, believeth all things, hopeth all things, endureth all things" (1 Co 13:7). Hopeth *all things*—even that a son or a daughter will do the right thing.

Children have a strong sense of fairness. Ask the average teenager, for example, "What do you think contributes most to the gap between you and your parents?" Many will answer, "They don't trust me. They nearly always expect the worst of me." Often, with an angry shrug, a teenager will echo Carl's words, "I might as well do it. I'll get blamed anyway."

How would you react to such treatment? I know how I would.

By contrast, there's a special quality about the child who knows that he is trusted. It tends to bring out the best in anyone when he has the assurance that people expect the best of him.

Our children know that we pray for them, but how much more our prayers mean when we exercise this "hopeth all things" faith in them. Fortunate is the child who, although his best doesn't quite come up to his mother's expectations, can rest assured that he will not be greeted with "Just a *B?* I knew you would never make the honor roll."

Such a mother must surely need a fresh touch from the One who, because He is incarnate love, "hopeth all things" for us.

4

Can We Afford Moods?

Mothers can't afford bad moods.

"Why not?" you may be asking. "Other people have bad moods."

Granted we all get up on the wrong side of the bed some mornings. So this is one of those days. Dad has been alerted before he arrives at the breakfast table. He monitors his words to keep peace.

Not so teenage Jack. Sensing the tension, he blurts out, "So Mom's in one of her moods!" Then, with the memory of other such occasions in his mind, he cautions his sister with a whispered, "Watch it, sis."

Breakfast is a fizzle, even though, with the contrariness with which we women seem to have been born, Mother has taken pains to prepare a particularly fine breakfast. One by one the members of the family go on their way for the day.

Alone, Mother begins to face reality. "Me and my moods," she says to herself with some disgust; and she begins to do some evaluating. "They've cost me the

13

loss of a happy, relaxed family starting the day together, eager chatter at the table, and loving good-bys. I'm beginning to think I can't afford these moods."

She's right, as I'm sure we all agree. Bad moods are definitely a luxury forbidden to the Christian. But how can we dispel them?

Since confession is good for the soul, let me share an experience of one such day in my life. Brought to the realization that I was in a particularly bad mood and increasingly convicted by the Holy Spirit, I dropped to my knees just where I was in my living room and asked the Lord to change my mood. It was a brief prayer; and as I rose from my knees, my eyes saw the lovely wood-grained wall motto with the heading "As a Man Thinketh." I read the scripture below it: "Whatsoever things are true, . . . honest, . . . just, . . . pure, . . . lovely; . . . think on these things" (Phil 4:8).

Think on these things. Since our moods are directly related to and regulated by our thoughts, following this scriptural advice is like waving a magic wand over a bad mood.

Can we afford moods? Yes, we can. We can afford *good* moods.

5

Focus on Creativity

Perhaps you know this family: their little girl displays almost genius quality in her art. Because of this unique ability she is protected and pampered.

"But your sister is drawing (or painting)," the mother explains as she shoos her son off to do some household chore. This mother brags of her daughter's creativity. Somehow she fails to read creativity into the precision with which her boy assembles and paints an intricate model plane, or the melt-in-your mouth brownies an older daughter makes "from scratch" for supper.

Sometimes it is unusual ability in music that sets one member of a family apart from the others. Hours are especially scheduled for practice for the musical member, while others in the family carry on with the pedestrian tasks.

Such discrimination generally produces two effects. First, the gifted child is caused "to think of himself more highly than he ought." He may grow up somewhat smug and tend to despise ability other than the

15

arts. This child needs to be helped to understand that not one of us has any talent or gift except what the Lord in His goodness has dispensed to us.

A second effect is that the so-called noncreative brother or sister may become resentful, resulting in his developing a cynical attitude toward all forms of art.

"What can I do? My child *is* gifted and unusually creative," a mother may say. Well, by all means she should encourage the gifted child to develop the gift, whether it be music or some other form of art. At the same time, however, she must see the creativity that fixes a splint for a wounded foundling sparrow, and the creativity in her small daughter's flower arrangement on the dining-room table (even when weeds may be the chief "flower" featured). She should be quick to spot creativity in a school project or in a batch of cookies—in anything that has a part of the person in it.

The boy or girl can be counted on to have the right kind of self-concept when an understanding mother, inspecting something the child has made or done, pronounces it good.

6

Practicing Acceptance

Wouldn't you agree that some of our children's most meaningful instruction comes in the course of life situations? Ten-year-old Philip, for example, learned one of life's lessons through the sheer delight of having a schoolfriend spend a weekend with him.

Making up the bunk beds, Philip's mother found to her horror, tucked underneath visitor Ted's pillow, an objectionable comic book. The boy knew that it had been discovered. What would you have done about the situation?

Ted is from a non-Christian home. We can't judge his actions by the standards we have taught our children. Many of the "how to" books say, "Accept, accept, accept." Does this mean that we're expected to close our eyes and, without demurring, let our child be exposed to such books?

What are some alternatives? One might be to play down the incident but to explain to our boy or girl why the book (or other offensive item) is not acceptable to us as Christians. Another solution would be to talk privately with the young guest, assuring him that he is welcome and that we want him to come often. Only after this assurance would we point out why we object to the comic book. I'm sure I need not suggest that it is the welfare of the boy himself that we would emphasize, rather than communicating a fear that our own child would be contaminated.

This is exactly how Philip's mother handled the situation. Let her tell the gratifying results.

"Ted listened while I explained—with an arm around his shoulder. Then, of his own accord, he took the book and tossed it into the wastebasket. He's a frequent visitor in our home, and he gladly attends Sunday school and church with us. We have the finest relationship."

Here is one fortunate boy who will not grow up "turned off" by the zealous but sometimes arrogant treatment of Christians in whose home he has been a guest.

Apart from the good effect on Ted, think how much Philip gained! He saw his mother in the best possible light. He learned from her how to maintain his Christian standards before his unsaved friends. Most of all, Philip learned that, although his mother rightly disapproved of an offensive book, she did not disapprove of Ted himself. This is one of the timeless lessons taught by the Saviour, who, while hating sin, loves the sinner.

7

Please Forgive Me

Some of us mothers grew up in an era of parental omnipotence. We were given to understand that our parents were virtually infallible. How could Mother or Dad ever say or do anything wrong?

Different, more realistic and sensible—and more scriptural—attitudes prevail in many Christian homes today. Correspondingly happier relationships are possible.

Let's think about this for a minute. How about using Mrs. A and Mrs. B as our examples? They are in the middle of a discussion.

Mrs. A (to her neighbor, Mrs. B): "Are you thinking about what it can do to your Billy to have his mother admit that she's made a mistake—and then to have you actually ask him to forgive you?"

Mrs. B: "What do you mean, '*Do* to him'?"

Mrs. A: "Aren't you afraid that he'll lose confidence in you—I mean, as an authority figure?"

Mrs. B (amazed): "I don't get it. You mean that to hear me say, 'I'm sorry, son. Will you please forgive me?' can possibly be a bad thing for Billy? No, I don't believe that!"

Mrs. A: "Well, that's how we've brought up our children, having them look up to us. How can they do this if we let them see that we're as prone to error as they are?"

Mrs. B: "You're kidding yourself. Children know that we make mistakes. I've tried to be honest with mine. Billy and Sue have heard me say 'Please forgive me' when it was in order. I don't feel this has robbed me of their respect or undermined their confidence in me."

The two women sit in silence for a few seconds. Then Mrs. B continues with a thoughtful expression on her face.

Mrs. B: "The authority figure I'm trying to establish for my boy and girl is the One who is the ultimate authority figure. My children hear me ask the Lord to forgive me for my sins and shortcomings. They have no illusions about my being infallible, believe me! But I'm praying that I can be the right kind of parent in helping them to look to God for forgiveness and to be willing to say 'Forgive me' to Him."

Mrs. A: "That puts a different light on it. I certainly want my children to feel that way about God, too." (She hesitates a moment.) "Do you suppose I've been reading the wrong books?"

Mrs. B: "Maybe so. I find my best child guidance in the Bible. For one thing, it never changes."

8

When the Real You Stands Up

Grace is a Sunday school teacher, and more than once she has told the young mothers in her class this story about herself.

"One time when I was asked to speak at a women's meeting, I chose as my topic, The Fruit of the Spirit. I enlarged on what the Bible says about each aspect—love, joy, peace, and all the rest of the ninefold fruit of the Spirit (Gal 5:22-23). I particularly dwelt on joy. I really went to town on that, speaking about the outward glow that proves the inner peace we have when the Holy Spirit dwells in us. I drew word pictures of the sad-faced creatures who do not have this inner joy to radiate on their faces, and what poor testimony they are to the power of God.

"Well, that message boomeranged! At the close of the meeting, a number of us went to a restaurant for a snack. After the waitress took our orders, she singled me out and said, 'I'll bring you a cup of tea right away. You look all worn out.' Me! All worn out so that it even showed on my face! After all my talk about peace and joy showing on the outside!"

Funny? Yes, if it were not so sadly true in our own lives, as many of us will admit. Grace is not alone in feeling that she had been saying one thing but doing another.

It's hard, though, to keep serene all day long when there are a hundred and one things to harry us. We tell our children to take their troubles to Jesus. Do we confuse children sometimes by our own lack of composure in the face of problems and difficulties, by the evident fact that we struggle with these matters ourselves instead of trusting the Lord to take care of them?

There's a sequel to Grace's story. Let her tell it.

"It was a steaming hot day. People were dragging themselves to the supermarket. On the street a neighbor, after commenting on the weather, said, 'You look so cool and nice. But then, you always do. You look as if you have an inner peace.'"

We may never be chagrined by the first situation that Grace shared with us, but wouldn't it be an encouragement to us to experience the second? We could be walking testimonies of God's grace.

9

Happy New Start!

Jean and Marilyn were chatting over their cups of coffee.

"Sometimes," Marilyn said with a wistful sigh, "I wish I could start all over."

"Me too," her neighbor agreed. "This morning, for instance!" She threw up her hands in a gesture that needed no words.

"I would be a better mother and a better wife, if only I could start out fresh," Marilyn pursued the subject. Jean's nod expressed complete understanding.

These two mothers are not alone. We would all admit at times to a desire to begin over—profiting from our previous mistakes, of course.

We can. Let's think about beginning anew. First, like Jean and Marilyn, we have to be dissatisfied with our present attitudes. Second, we must have the determination that today is the day for change. Then we tackle each area, one at a time. But we should set no discouragingly impossible goals of instant perfection.

By the way, there's nothing wrong with scoring yourself on your efforts and small successes. Were you cheerful even before the first cup of coffee this morning? Ten points. Did you stifle a yell at Junior when he wakened the baby? Another ten. Instead of haranguing your teenage daughter with "You're not eating after all the trouble I've gone to for you!" did you encourage her by asking, "Can I do something to help so you'll have time to eat, honey?" Extra points for this. No points, though, for stopping to listen as Tommy dashes in and breathlessly recites his day's adventures. You're already rewarded with his big smile and his exclamation, "Mom, you're really listening!" The attention given to what he is saying assures the boy that he is important to his mother.

Evening comes; and because we have talked with God throughout the day, sharing with Him our problems and cares, we no longer greet our husbands with some nagging recital of our difficult day, such as may have marred many of his previous homecomings.

Does this sound altogether unrealistic? All at once, it undoubtedly is; but progressive starting over again isn't an unattainable goal.

Beginning with such an understandng, we will realize eventually that we are doing nothing less than producing some of the fruit of the Spirit. Who knows? We may ultimately find ourselves with a whole basket of fruit grown one at a time—beginning with this happy new start!

10

One Day at a Time

One of my favorite poems is Annie Johnson Flint's "One Day at a Time." Maybe it's because I have a short-term endurance, or, as the experts call it, a low frustration tolerance.

Without a doubt, the Lord must have had in mind this weakness of His creatures when He gave us the reassuring promise, "As thy days, so shall thy strength be" (Deu 33:25).

Not weeks or months or years—the promise is for one day at a time.

This truth may not have too much meaning for us until we come to a day that finds us, at the end of it, completely exhausted. We've struggled along on our own. Night finds us sighing, "I can't drag myself around another minute. I'm out of it."

We all feel like this at times. We can take comfort in the thought that although tomorrow's duties, seen from tonight's perspective, appear just too much to cope with, when tomorrow comes, with it will also come the promised strength for the new day.

Better than all the promises of the vitamin compounders with their glorified advertising of pills that will assure us of boundless energy all day long, is the sure Word of our God.

How wise He is in giving to us this needed strength one day at a time! We might be tempted to dissipate it if He were to dispense it to us by the week or by the month.

This strength that God has promised is not a static amount, not a "that's it and you have to make do with it" portion. No! It is "as thy days"—according to the special need of the particular day—that God grants to us the enabling strength. What a blessing that is! The supply never runs short.

So, if today we've run out of steam and used up all our energy, we'll just rise in the morning and remind God in our prayers of His promise for the day.

> One day at a time, and the day is His day;
> He hath numbered its hours, though they haste or
>   delay;
> His grace is sufficient; we walk not alone;
> As the day, so the strength that He giveth His
>   own.

We owe it to ourselves and to our families to accept from God this poise-producing daily strength. Isn't this a better idea than trying to go it alone, making each day a kind of endurance test?

11

Time to Do Nothing

A mother of five children, whom I knew for just a brief period one summer, impressed me unforgettably with this thought: "I think that everybody has to have time to do nothing." She went on to explain, "I like my own children to have some time to do nothing."

In this hectic, active, get-with-it generation, time to do *nothing?*

This mother showed great insight in recognizing that the desire to have and to enjoy more leisure time is a need of all ages. It can take different forms. Your usually active teenager may sit on the front steps alone, his head cupped in his hands and not a muscle moving. Your five-year-old may stand by the window staring out, strangely quiet. But they are not really doing nothing. The teen may be, in the words of the Arabs, "letting his soul catch up with his body." He may be sorting out the threads of a tangled problem.

As wise, sensitive mothers, we don't intrude and suggest, "Shouldn't you be getting busy?" Nor do we com-

27

plain, "Is *that* all you have to do?" The reward for understanding this need to do nothing might very well be a gratifying sharing, a heart response from a son or a daughter.

Five-year-old Ginny stood quite still for several minutes. In silence she watched the fine rain trickle down the window. Then she turned wide-eyed to her mother and said, "Mommie, I was just thinking—maybe Jesus will come soon." In her moments of doing nothing, this child's mind had turned from the toys of time to the joys of eternity.

By respecting these quiet times we will be given a glimpse of the thoughts that enrich our children's lives. We must make allowance for a time to do nothing.

Is this, perhaps, something of what the Scripture has in mind in the injunction to "study to be quiet" (1 Th 4:11)?

We all catch ourselves doing nothing. It may be when we are momentarily gazing out the window as the potato lies unpeeled in our hands or when standing seemingly idle by the washing machine or ironing board. Why should we feel a sense of guilt at such times?

Mothers, too, need a time to do nothing—for soul expansion.

12

"Spoon-lickin' Good"

"There's no law that says a medicine has to taste bad in order to make you feel good," stated a clever television commercial.

Anne Blaine was reminded of this one day last winter. She approached the bed where her son was confined with a virus cold. In her hand were a bottle and a spoon. She saw Mike's face draw into an anticipatory grimace, but it soon brightened in amazement.

"Hey, Mom!" he exclaimed, licking the last of the contents of the spoon. "This tastes so good I don't see how it can help me get out of here fast."

Long before the era of television, David the psalmist had voiced the same sentiment: "See, how good and how pleasant it is for brothers to live harmoniously together!" (Ps 133:1, Berkeley).

How good *and* how pleasant. This is surely what the Lord planned for us as Christians. Just as certainly He expects that we will project this kind of positive faith. Maybe some of us will have to back up and begin to erase the deep-seated idea that what is spiritually good for a person cannot possibly give pleasure, that living for Christ is a grim business not to be confused with fun and laughter and the good things of life. Such ideas have sparked the long-faced Christian image. When this is "the taste" that all too many children and young people have been offered, it's no wonder that so few go on to be the "blessed" who put their trust in God (Ps 34:8).

Along with our earnest prayer that our sons and daughters will not become spiritual dropouts—one of those who say defiantly, "I can hardly wait to get away from home and all that religious stuff"—perhaps we should take stock of the brand of Christianity they have been sampling at home.

Are we majoring on the negative, frowning on the children's desires to do some things that we didn't do ourselves—things that are not necessarily undesirable, just new? Mrs. Billy Graham, speaking at a women's luncheon, confessed to having learned a lesson along this line. Hearing what she thought was a loud rock and roll record, she put her foot down. "Off with that noise!" she commanded. Rethinking her action, she asked some questions about the particular type of music and even made a point of purchasing a similar record which was a favorite of one of her children.

"My reward," she related with a warm smile, "was that I was invited to sit down and listen to the new record." The generation gap had been bridged.

30

Isn't this the kind of consideration that will cause our children to think that spirituality can be *both* good and pleasant? In fact, it can be "spoon-lickin' good."

13

A Realistic Concept

Once I heard of a woman who was privileged to attend a specialized group meeting. "Even though I'm just a housewife and mother," she stated, apparently overwhelmed by the honor of being selected.

How would you describe yourself? As "just a housewife," or "just a mother" (or both)? The life to which the average, normal female aspires from the time she cradles a doll or serves pretend tea and cookies from her toy dishes! To be sure our work is largely nonglamorous; it's mundane and often menial, with a never-ending regularity of doing things that bring no glory to us. This, however, is what we do, it is not what we are. We need to differentiate between the two.

Other people—our own family included—will regard us in the light of the image that we project to them.

One of the most poised, well-adjusted women I have ever met does housework to earn her living. She could so easily think of herself as "just a cleaning woman." But does she? No! With the utmost naturalness she

32

says to the career women who employ her, "You have your profession and I have mine." She has a right concept of herself, not fuzzied by what her work might make her think of herself.

"Don't think of yourself too highly," the Scripture exhorts us (Ro 12:3). But does that give us license to think of ourselves too lowly? Keep in mind that we are God's workmanship, created in His image, redeemed and made fit to stand in His presence through the shed blood of His Son: this will give us a true perspective of ourselves.

Just a housewife. Just a mother. Have you pondered the fact that God needs housewives and mothers more than He needs almost any of the professionals whose positions we're so prone to set above our humble place in our homes?

That gives a dignity to the daily chores. As we consider that we are in vital partnership with God, surely not one of us will ever be guilty of thinking of ourselves as "just a—." We will take our position with other women who are not as fortunate as we in many instances and who, if the truth were known, might gladly trade places with any one of us in our homes. With pride we'll let it be known that we are indeed mothers and homemakers.

14

No Excuses, Please

Over ten o'clock coffee, Alice and her neighbor, Joan, listened to their favorite radio preacher.

"Now that's a new concept to me," said Joan, furrowing her brow in deep thought. " 'God does not excuse us.' Is that what you understood him to say?"

"Right," Alice agreed, "but it's new to me too!"

With a quizzical look on each face, the girls listened as the speaker continued:

". . . when God forgives, He forgives us outright. No strings attached. Not the way we forgive each other so often by excusing what the other has done. What I mean is, we say something like, 'You were tired (or busy or something else)'; and the person doesn't feel forgiven. He feels inferior for not having been able to overcome the tiredness or the pressure or whatever excuse you make for his failure or shortcoming."

"Well, if that isn't something to think about," exclaimed Alice. "I never would have thought of it, but it's true. I do it all the time."

"I'm afraid I have to admit to the same," sighed Joan, "and especially with the children. I never realized I was doing this, not giving them the feeling that I forgave them."

Perhaps you've had this experience. You've said or done something only to be sorry about it; and you've said, "Please forgive me." Then the person whom you have offended or wronged says exactly what this radio preacher explained: "Of course I forgive you. After all, you were tired (or something else); that accounted for the words or actions."

How uncomfortable this leaves us. Sort of put down by the other person while he or she appears so magnanimous for being understanding and forgiving.

Children see through this. They discern real forgiveness that doesn't take into consideration all the periphera: forgiveness that blots out the offence and leaves the offender with his self-respect before the forgiver.

> Be ye kind one to another . . . forgiving one another, even as God for Christ's sake hath forgiven you (Eph 4:32).

This is the scriptural variety of forgiveness—in its full measure, with no excusing to nullify the forgiveness, no belittling of the other person.

How about testing ourselves in the light of the radio preacher's concept of forgiveness?

15

Too Young to Decide

"We do all the deciding for our family," Gloria stated in the course of a discussion on the subject of decision-making. "After all," she justified her remark, "why should we let our teenagers do this? How can we expect them to be smart enough or wise enough to know what they're doing? They'll almost certainly end up making the wrong decision and being sorry for it."

Should there be just one school of thought in this instance, or would it be good for us to ponder this mother's view before accepting it?

First, would you agree that there's a certain smugness about her words, "We (I assume she was including her husband)do all the deciding"? It smacks of "We never make a wrong decision," don't you think? I find myself wondering where and when this young mother learned how to make a good decision in every situation.

Then her question, "Why should we let the children—in this instance, teenagers—decide?" Why? How else will they learn what they will have to live with throughout their entire lives: that the right to make a decision

36

carries with it the responsibility to live with the consequences of one's decision?

Don, not yet in his teens, was faced with this alternative: accept the invitation of an uncle who offered to take him to a fine summer camp, or remain at home where he was almost certain to excel in a day camp Field Day, to which he had looked forward for weeks and for which he had diligently trained.

"The choice almost tore him apart," related his understanding parents, "but it had to be Don's own decision. He wavered between one and the other alternative until the final day for booking his flight to camp. It was his decision. He had to live with it. He decided to go away to camp, and it turned out to be one of his happiest experiences."

Even young children can be taught to make decisions. Five-year-old Mary may be given the right to choose which of three dresses she wishes to wear. Not a confusing, unlimited selection, but one made within set guidelines.

When the big choices of life come, fortunate is the person whose parents fostered in him the ability to make a good decision. We can be certain that this is God's intent, for in this, our ability to reason and make a choice, that we differ from all lower creation.

So should we not pause and think of the consequences in the lives of the children God has entrusted to us, before doggedly determining that "We (or I) make all the decisions for the family"?

16

The Solution That Worked

John isn't a typical teenager. Everyone who knows him agrees he's the worst, the very worst. His mother has two problems, for her sixth grade daughter laments over and over, "Mom! I wish John was anybody's brother but mine. You don't know how awful it is when the kids keep saying to me, 'D'you know what your brother's done now?'"

John's parents tried everything. Then one day at a Christian women's club luncheon, his mother remarked, "After hearing that outstanding young man speak, I surely would like to talk to his mother." The wish was quickly granted for the speaker's mother was seated at the same table as John's mother. The two were soon engaged in conversation. Asked if she could suggest a solution for dealing with John, the mother of the speaker shared the experience she had had with another of her sons.

"He was everything you tell me your boy is. Almost always in some kind of trouble, yet such a loveable, generous-natured kid, and so ready to ask our forgiveness. But he just seemed to be unable to stay out of trouble. We were at our wits' end. We had tried punishment in every form that we thought would affect him for the better. Nothing worked. We prayed earnestly. Even that did no apparent good.

"Did you ever manage to get through to him. Did he ever change?"

"Oh, yes, he did. Let me tell you."

All the ladies at the table were listening keenly now.

"It came to me one day when Tim was about to leave for school. He was an affectionate boy and would never leave without kissing me goodbye. That day, as I stood at the door with him, I put my hands on his shoulders and prayed something like this:

"Dear Lord, You know my boy's heart. You know he doesn't mean to get into trouble and that he's always sorry afterwards. Will You please remind him today, when he is tempted to do something he shouldn't, that I'm praying for him."

"Did it work?" a chorus of voices asked.

"It wasn't some kind of magic. Tim didn't suddenly turn angelic. But from that day on, as I prayed with him, there was a change. Before the month was out his teachers were remarking about it. The real reassurance came, though, the day his sister said, 'Mom! Whatever's happened to Tim? The kids are all getting to like him, and know what? I'm kinda glad he's my brother, after all.'"

39

"Please, God," said John's mother reverently, "I'll hear my daughter say the same." She turned with misty eyes and extended her hand to the mother of the speaker. "I'm going home to practice what you've taught me," she promised.

17

The Middle Kid

Let's think of a family where there are three, five or seven children. Your own may be such a family, in fact.

Naturally, when a family, after the first child, consists of an uneven number of children, there is the inevitable middle child. Middle children all too frequently have unique problems which tend to reach crisis proportions in the teens.

It appears that the problem is most acute in the three-child family, even when the mother conscientiously tries to guard against any form of favoritism. There is the firstborn, the family pride and joy; then there is the baby, the pet and darling of parents, grandparents, cousins, and aunts; and somewhere in between, neither old enough nor young enough for special favors, is the middle child.

Have you heard some mothers refer to a child as "my middle son or daughter"? One mother so consistently introduced the second of her three sons as "our middle boy" that he began to so identify himself when he answered the telephone in his home, as though his only identity was to be found in relationship to his brothers.

How can a mother, sensitive to her child's needs in this direction, compensate? One way is to refrain from considering his position in the family as a standard of behavior for him. No more "You know you're not old enough for that kind of thing," and the confusing opposite "At your age you should know better."

The insightful mother will also point up the particular abilities of this child, making him or her feel important and causing him to stand out from the older and younger members of the family.

If it appears that we're putting too much stress on the feelings of the middle child, perhaps we should remind ourselves that our children will take with them into the world the attitudes bred in the home. How important, then, that they feel accepted for themselves, not shadowed by either an older or a younger brother or sister.

Aren't you glad that God has no "middle children"; that we are equally precious in His sight; that He is no respecter of persons (Acts 10:34)? Pondering this comforting truth, will we determine that no discrimination will be shown in our family?

That boy or girl in the middle may never have expressed his feelings, but we can be certain that he will begin to be aware that Mom is working on the solution to his problems.

Studies show that some of these children are difficult

to challenge to worthwhile activity because, in their opinion, they have so much to overcome. The concerned mother can make a life-changing contribution to her middle child when she is no respecter of persons.

18

Do We Have to Be Late All the Time?

Thirteen-year-old Jerry confided to his aunt who was visiting, "I wish Mom didn't take so long to get ready. She makes us kids late so often that I'm embarrassed. Everybody looks at me when I come in late to class every Sunday."

The understanding relative listened then commented, "Your mother looks so lovely, though, when she does get ready, Jerry."

He nodded agreement to that. "I'm proud of Mom. He sighed, "But I just wish we could be on time."

Are you saying, "It's all right for my son to complain; but *I'm* the one who has to get breakfast, see that the younger ones are dressed for Sunday school, and start preparations for dinner. No wonder I'm a little late"?

Nevertheless, the young teenager has a well-taken point. To be sure, there is little to be said for the mother who gets the family there on time regardless of her own appearance. How commendable it is though to so organize and plan that (barring emergencies) we manage to be both punctual and attractive. The time differential can be just minutes usually. Sadly, once we begin to be late, it tends to become a habit. And who wants to be known as "the late Browns" or whatever the name.

The detestable name is earned gradually: one minute late, two minutes, five—then, what's the use? Nobody expects your family to be on time. And all the while a teenager is suffering intensely.

Happily, "As long as a person is breathing, he can change," to quote Dr. C. M. Narramore, psychologist. Wouldn't next Sunday be a good time to make the change? What a pleasure, then, to hear your teenager exclaim, "Mom! We're on time. Do I feel good about this!"

Actually, when it's a matter of habitual tardiness at church, not only do we embarrass our family but we are causing them to establish a bad habit which they may carry on throughout life. Far worse, however, is the attitude that can so readily insult God Himself by presuming to consider it unimportant whether or not we are in time for worship services.

No doubt young Jerry's gripe comes under the category of "parents provoking your children to wrath" (Eph 6:4), and Scripture is on Jerry's side in this instance. Surely, when a mother becomes aware of her son's feelings in this matter, she'll find ways to save minutes and make him proud of his mom who looks great and is on time.

19

Hoisting the Stop Sign

You walk your first grader to the busy intersection and leave him there, safe in the care of the school traffic officer. It may be that you recognize this lady. Out of uniform she is just like you, one of the neighborhood mothers.

You watch for a minute as she shepherds the group of children to safety, then you hurry home. Are you thinking, "She's welcome to her job, out in the cold and rain when she's not sweltering in the heat"? Or, are you impressed that not only the traffic—and there's plenty of it at that time of morning—but the kids of whatever age unquestioningly obey this woman? She steps out into the intersection, her STOP sign hoisted; and she is instantly master of the situation.

Worth considering, isn't it?

This dogmatic, uncompromising person! How many accidents to schoolchildren has she prevented? How many deaths?

"Who does she think she is?" questions a motorist waiting for her sanction before he can proceed. Who is she? A representative of the state with all the authority of the state behind her. So, in the name of authority she lowers her STOP sign and waves her hand for GO.

Does the allegory present itself to your mind?

As mothers, there are times when for the safety of a child we have no alternative but to hoist our STOP sign. Not only has God made us responsible for the safety of our children—eternal as we seek to lead them to Christ and temporal in that we set safe boundaries for them— but He has given us all the authority of heaven while we are on duty.

"I just wish my children would obey me like they obey the school traffic officer," you might be saying. Can it be that they understand why she is doing what she does and that sometimes, at home, this is not so? "Never mind asking why. Just do what I tell you because I'm your mother," we frequently hear. And the unwilling child comes as near to disobeying as he dares. Maybe if we took a moment to explain the "why he should" and the consequences if he does otherwise, we would foster a more cooperative attitude on the part of our children.

Nevertheless, there will be times when, in the interests of our child, as good stewards of the one God has entrusted to us, we will uncompromisingly hoist the STOP sign.

Having heeded the exhortation of the wise man of the

Bible (Pr 22:6), we can confidently claim for our child that "when he is old, he will not depart from it."

The child so trained will hoist his own STOP signs as he grows through the teen years into manhood.

20

A Little Bit Like God

To say Mike's mother was surprised is putting it too mildly, when he came out with, "Mom! Why can't you be just a little bit like God?"

She stopped in the middle of dropping cookies onto the sheet and said, "What d'you mean?" Then, to gain a minute to recapture her composure, she added, "Do you have to be so irreverent, Michael Green?"

"What do I mean?" he parroted his mother's question. "Well, I don't want to hurt your feelings or anything, Mom; but remember what we read this morning about when we ask God to forgive us, He sort of buries our sins and He doesn't keep bringing them up every time we do something else and have to ask forgiveness for that too."

After a long pause, Mrs. Green said thoughtfully, "I see, son. I know what you mean."

It didn't take much concentration for her to recall some instances that justified her teenager's gripes. Recently he had come home later than was permitted and had been deprived of a privilege. A few days later, a different offence and—"I can hear myself." She shook her head in annoyance at her own behavior, remembering her words, "Mike, you know I haven't forgotten the other day when you—"

To her mind came something she had read from the life of Susanna Wesley. One of her rules, or as Susanna called the procedure, "Recipe for Raising Children," was "No child should be punished twice for the same fault and he should not be upbraided with it afterwards."

If it seems like irreverence to presume to be "a little bit like God," surely this would be one of the most pardonable instances. We sing

> What a wondrous blessing in God's Word,
> My sins are blotted out, I know.

How would we feel if, every time we confessed a sin or shortcoming to God, He reminded us that we were still on probation for the last time we confessed? Part of the glory of our relationship with God our Father is His assurance, "I, even I, am he that blotteth out thy transgressions for mine own sake, and will not remember thy sins" (Is 43:25).

Maybe we can all benefit from Mike's suggestion to his mother. Who of us wouldn't want to be considered by our son or daughter "a little bit like God"? Think of the privilege a mother has of clarifying the image of God

rather than completely distorting the image created
initially by the Word of God. It's in our power to "up"
the image of God. Yes, it is!

21

How's Your Homework, Mom?

Between bites of an after-school snack, Jerry Blake turned to his mother with the question, "Mom, what's an Ebenezer?"

Taken off guard, Joan Blake exclaimed, "A *what,* son?"

"An Ebenezer," Jerry repeated. "You know, we sing, 'Here I raise my Ebenezer.'"

A warm, understanding smile lit up his mother's face. "Oh! Now I know what you mean. You had me puzzled for a minute."

She stopped her dinner preparations and sat down across the kitchen from her son. She had no idea what had prompted the question in her eleven-year-old boy's mind, but obviously he deserved an explanation. But where to begin. She started to hum the tune involuntarily.

"That's it, Mom," and Jerry whistled along with his mother's humming of "Come, Thou Fount of Every

Blessing," a line of which had sparked his question about *Ebenezer*.

"We have to think about the line that follows to get our clue as to the meaning of the word," she began her explanation. "It says, 'Hither by Thy help I'm come.' Or we would say, by God's help I've arrived where I am today. But for the background, we have to look in the Bible rather than the hymnbook."

Together they searched in a concordance in the back of Jerry's Bible, then turned to 1 Samuel 7:10-12. Eagerly Jerry read the verses then commented, "It's like a monument, isn't it, Mom, to remember that God helped them when they specially needed Him?"

Satisfied with the answer to his question, Jerry was off to do his homework before supper.

Watching him take the steps three at a time, his mother pondered a moment then prayed, "Thank You, Lord, for letting me do this bit of homework for You."

Sometimes our homework takes one form, sometimes another. These days with new math, new grammar, and a whole range of space-age subjects that are foreign to some of us with our preatomic education, we have to admit to ignorance of much that our children are studying. One subject, however, is unchanging; and God looks to mothers to go into partnership with Him.

What more rewarding homework can we ever busy ourselves with than that of making Bible truth come alive for our own children? How wonderful to know they are growing up to commemorate their own Ebe-

53

nezers, to build their personal monuments in gratitude
to and in acknowledgement of the God who helps when
they specially need Him!

22

Sorry for What?

"Sorry, Mommie." The phrase is lisped early with or without meaning. This is innocent enough in babyhood. Mouthed later, it can become a glib, meaningless term.

Let's chat a little bit about what "I'm sorry" can connote.

Is it "sorry for what I did"?

Is it "sorry I was caught doing it"?

The first law of nature is self-preservation, so it figures that our children learn early that saying "I'm sorry" is an escape route from the consequences of punishable behavior. So we need to teach them just as early in life what *being sorry* really means. Perhaps in our own lives we can look back on occasions when to our young minds all that seemed to matter to Mother was that we said, "I'm sorry" (you'll stay in your room until you do), yet our memory doesn't recall the particular sin or shortcoming related to the incident. We would not want our children to grow up with such fuzzy values, would we?

Our teenagers with their great capacity for fairness especially react to such treatment by becoming resentful. They profit much more from a direct spelling out of what they have done or left undone.

Sometimes we may be guilty of not letting our child explain before we denounce him or her. Let me share a true illustration. Janey, all dressed up, started to go to a friend's birthday party. Moments later back she came, her pretty dress looking a sight. Rather fearfully she opened the kitchen door. Her mother took one look and said, "Whatever happened, honey?" and reached to help Janey take off the dress. The loving treatment brought on a flood of tears, and between sobs the little girl said, "Oh, Mommie! Jesus answered my prayer. You're not mad at me. I'm awful sorry 'bout my dress."

This mother had taught her children to take their troubles to Jesus, telling them that He does answer a child's prayer. What would this little girl have thought of her mother's Saviour if the mother herself had not been understanding, if she had not let the child explain that actually she had not been careless but that a passing car had splashed mud on her clothes?

A daily consciousness that many times we have to say, "I'm sorry, Lord," gives us this kind of insight into how God would have us treat our own children. And together we grow spiritually and with understanding and compassion for one another.

23

The Little Mimic

One of the most poignant stories I ever heard was this: four-year-old Martha, hugging a doll in each of her pudgy little arms, looks wistfully up at her mother and says, "Mommie, I love them and love them and love them, and they *never love me back.*"

Doesn't this tug at your heart? What an unparalleled opportunity for a mother to explain how much Jesus loves every one of us and how He longs for us to return His love.

There is another side, a warm, lovely side, to the homey scene of the child with her dolls. Where, do you suppose, did Martha learn the art of loving? Without a doubt, here is a child who lives secure in the knowledge that she herself is loved. We can imagine a mother who spontaneously takes a moment now and again throughout each day to express her love, and just as certainly she is rewarded by a returned hug. Otherwise why would her little daughter expect this response from her dolls when she "loves them and loves them"?

We all have had occasion to observe our own behavior mirrored in the actions of our children, sometimes as they have played with their dolls and toys, sometimes in their attitudes towards their playmates. The boy whose mother yells at him yells at younger children, including his own younger brothers or sisters. Conversely, there's a gentleness, a lack of belligerence in the relaxed, well-adjusted child who knows he is loved by his parents.

It does shake us up sometimes when we see and hear ourselves in the actions and words of our children. Would that we could say to our children of whatever age, "Those things, which ye have both learned, and received, and heard, and seen in me, do" (Phil 4:9*a*).

"But that was the apostle Paul," I can hear someone sigh.

Yes, Paul, the fiery, dogmatic, unloving bigot whom an encounter with Christ changed into the Christian who could dare issue this directive.

For a healthy spiritual exercise we should ask ourselves and answer with complete honesty, "Just how much of what they see and hear and learn from me dare I suggest that my children copy?" Is your list discouragingly small? Let it be a challenge to chalk up new areas that will be a fine example for your children to follow.

One thing we need never be afraid of is having our child mimic us in being kind and loving to others, beginning in our own home.

24

Decisions, Decisions, Decisions

I flipped the pictorial calendar as September slipped into history; and there, superimposed on a reproduction of one of God's fall masterpieces, were the words:

> Cause me to hear thy lovingkindness in the morning; for in thee do I trust; cause me to know the way wherein I should walk; for I lift up my soul unto thee (Ps 143:8).

It was the phrase "Cause me to know the way" that grabbed my interest, for no one is more likely to be in need of this kind of assurance.

There are some women who appear to have been born with their minds made up, with the faculty of being able to arrive at a decision that takes the rest of us much longer—if we ever do! I must admit to belonging in the latter category. Maybe you do too.

To be sure, major decisions properly are the province of the head of the house, and ideally many decisions are the result of a family council. We all know, however, that each day brings its quota of decision-making for a mother. Our decisions may not be earth-shaking; but, once made, they have to be lived with.

How glad we can be for such verses as greeted me on my October calendar and inspire such hymns as

> I will guide thee; I will guide thee;
> I will guide thee with mine eye.

Only the Lord who created us knows us, knows the weaknesses that call for His special wisdom in added measure. Nothing is more confidence-inspiring than the sense that, having sought God's direction (and inherent in this prayer is our admission, "Lord, I don't know. I'm not competent to make this decision alone"), we can proceed on the basis of the facts at hand at the time. Subsequent information may cause us to wonder, "Was that the right decision?" We will never know, for as a wise man has written, "History does not reveal its alternatives." Nevertheless, we rely on the One whose name is Counselor and Guide. What more could we ask to aid us?

Since many of our decisions vitally relate to our children and can materially influence them both now and in the future, we cannot—we dare not—leave God out of our decisions.

25

Please Let Them Read

"Chris wants nothing to do with athletics. All he wants to do is read, read, read." A defensive note mixed with the complaint in Sally's voice as she described her son's interests.

Perhaps you've been a listener to such a conversation. One mother brags of her child's prowess in sports: baseball, football, track, swimming or tennis. Others add their story of a child's ability in some athletic activity. It's easy to detect the reflected glory enjoyed by the proud mamas.

By contrast, there are the kids who couldn't care less who wins what in any competitive sport. And their mothers are strangely sensitive to the situation.

Why do we get upset if a boy or girl chooses to spend leisure time in reading or in pursuing a nonathletic interest such as science or some form of art? Can our world be run by the sports greats?

Naturally we want our children to be well balanced, and the Bible speaks of bodily exercise profiting (a little). The child who fits into the sports image (a boy particularly) will doubtless have an easy time with his peers, everything else being equal.

What, then, of the reflective young reader who goes on to use the knowledge acquired through extracurricular reading? Our world needs poets as well as ballplayers. Do you recall the case of Isaac Watts? As a child, it is said that he constantly angered his father because of his natural ability to rhyme. At last the father forbade his six-year-old to speak in rhyme and meter on penalty of severe punishment. The boy faced his dad and said,

> Oh, father dear, do pity take;
> And I no verses more will make.

How many timeless hymns would never have been written had Isaac Watts' father not relented.

Likewise, our world needs scientists more than it needs sportsmen.

So, if God sends into your home a child with a penchant for reading, perhaps He is giving you the privilege of raising a boy or a girl who will one day serve the Lord in ways that will distinguish the child as he grows to manhood, in ways that will give your child a place in life that will bring blessing to others.

Will we encourage rather than frown on our young readers? This will put us in the company of Paul, who exhorted Timothy, his son in the faith, "Till I come, give attendance to reading" (1 Ti 4:13).

26

Male or Female

Sex education: long a taboo, now an out-in-the-open topic.

Like many another young mother, Joan had thought from time to time how she would tackle the subject when her little Tommy raised it.

He was a second grader when one day after school she sensed the time had come. Impatiently Tommy asked, "Mom, what am I?"

Joan sat her little boy down and, in the manner of all the instruction she had ever had, began to explain a few simple biological facts. Tommy was unimpressed. Moreover he was distinctly wriggly and anxious to be off playing. After a few minutes he slid off the end of the bench in the breakfast nook, very obviously not satisfied with his mother's explanation. His "What am I?" was still unanswered as far as he was concerned.

"Mom! All I have to know is, am I an *M* or an *F*? We have to put this on the paper the teacher gave us. So what am I?"

"Oh!" Joan sighed in relief then broke into laughter. "You're an *M*, son. Now run off and play 'til supper."

During the week Joan mentioned the incident to a few other mothers in the neighborhood and found that she was not alone in her initial bungling in trying to enlighten her son as to the facts of life.

"I've come to the conclusion," a mother of three shared with the others, "that the best thing is to be honest and answer just the question the child asks at the time. Not hedging or giving out with fanciful tales such as I was told. A child appreciates a straight answer, and this honesty will cause them to come to us rather than go to someone else as other questions arise in their minds."

"I agree," another mother chipped in. "And after all, we should be the ones to tell our children about God's wonderful plan for bringing a baby into the world, making the whole subject beautiful and reverent."

"Then we don't have to be afraid of what they might learn from other kids," Joan added. "I'll try to be more prepared for Tommy's question the next time, so I won't confuse or bore him with answers to questions he's not asking." She laughed at the remembrance.

"I like what we've been saying about *honest answers*," the youngest of the mothers commented thoughtfully. "I've read in the Bible something about 'providing things honest' but I have to admit that I've failed there. I'm more interested in a quick answer to get off the subject."

It was a good thing for all of us that Tommy brought up the question of male or female, Joan," one mother concluded; and the others nodded their agreement.

27

You Can Afford It

Speaking at a mother and daughter banquet, the mother of five children shared her formula for raising her children to be happy, well-adjusted Christian boys and girls.

"It's love," she said, "love all the way." Then, with the air of someone arriving at the punch line, she leaned toward her audience and added, "And *you can afford it.*"

Observing this lady, poised, radiating warmth, her eyes fun-filled at times, I thought, *She's for real. The love she advocates is the kind that works.*

Is it any wonder that of her five children four are already serving God in creative, fulfilling missionary service, and the fifth, a teenager, evidences similar goals for his life.

Have we, perhaps, in our harried efforts to provide more and more *things* as we can afford them, neglected this potent factor?

A mother who had been left as a fairly young woman

to bring up her three small boys, said one day, "My boys haven't had the things they wanted always. I haven't been able to do for them all I would like to have done, but one thing I know is that *they've had all the love they could take."*

I know this home. God is intensely real to each of these growing boys. There's freedom and fun in the family. They pray together and sing together. They're in no doubt as to where their mother's strength comes from: they see her on her knees; they hear her praying for them. Griping at each other is unknown. "All the love they can take" is working its magic in their lives, compensating for other lacks.

True love encompasses all the other virtues; and this mother diligently teaches her sons the blessings of obedience, consideration for others, thankfulness, the joy of simple things, the fruit of the Spirit.

Practicing this kind of love in the home costs a mother a lot in time and patience—but you can afford it. In fact, you can afford it so much more than you cannot afford it.

It should give Christians food for sober thought that it has taken some young people *outside* the church in this generation to focus attention on the great, universal heart hunger for love.

We have enough and to spare. Let's *afford* it.

28

More than One Way

Second-grader Judy came dashing into the living room just in time to hear her junior-high brother, David, say, "It's all set then, Mom? Craig can go with us tonight and stay over 'til morning?"

Before the mother could reply, Judy danced up and down. "Goody!" she said with glee. "I like when we have friends in for overnight." Then, as though a specially delightful thought had struck her, she added, "an' Craig can have devotions with us at breakfast, too."

David drew in his breath quickly. "Do we— I mean, couldn't we skip devotions just this once?"

"Not have our devotions!" Judy's tone made it sound as though she had never heard such an unacceptable suggestion.

What would you do in this situation? A sensitive young teenager, a believer in Christ, yet hesitant to expose his non-Christian friend to family devotions. The little sister, newly saved, a Good News Club-er, an ardent little witness for Christ. Both deserve your understanding and consideration.

It would be interesting to know how you would handle the situation; but, in the meantime, let's think of some of the ramifications.

You decide to make no changes in the family schedule because of your son's guest. After all, aren't family devotions the most meaningful part of your day as a family? And if Craig doesn't like it, he needn't come again. David surely has other friends!

You would like to leave the door open to "play it by ear" when morning comes. But there is Judy looking up at you with eyes that fairly accuse you if you dare think of such a thing. And there is God's Word: "Them that honour me I will honour" (1 Sa 2:30).

No way around that—or is there, in this case? Which is more honoring to God—to exhibit to a stranger a family who love each other enough that they can be flexible, or to doggedly pursue the program of the day?

One mother I know managed to come up with a happy combination.

At breakfast, when the family had guests whom they were praying for and witnessing to, instead of the family Bible and a devotional book, a copy of *Good News for Modern Man* was brought out and a chapter read.

"You mean you're reading the Bible!" a teenage guest exclaimed in amazement. "Read some more," she requested.

The host and hostess exchanged glances that said, "There's more than one way to conduct our family devotions."

29

Everyone Likes to Feel Special

What do you do when one of your children snuggles up to you saying, "Mommie, do you love me best? Peggy says you love her best. You don't, do you, Mommie?"

A conundrum for a mother. A chance to be as wise as Solomon.

Here's how one mother handled this bid for first place in her affections. When her younger child came with the plea, she assured her, "Honey, you're my favorite little girl and Helen is my favorite big girl," and the little one smiled with satisfaction.

It does seem childish, but everyone has to feel special to someone else. As adults we don't express ourselves as openly as a child but the longing is there, so we can empathize with our child's bid for acceptance and attention.

Sometimes it takes a success experience to make a child feel good about himself and acceptable to other people. It's important, then, that we watch for signs of a particular ability in each of our children. One has a good singing voice. Another is artistic and creative. When one child is especially talented and receives abundant applause and attention, the other children in the family may suffer by comparison unless the mother is sensitive to their feelings and does something to compensate. It's when this is not done that the little one pleads for assurance of our love.

Aren't you glad that, far more than you can ever convince your children of your love, God gives us assurance that we are special to Him. God has no favorites. We are accepted in the Beloved (Eph 1:6).

Sometimes it appears that God does have favorites. Can it be that these are the people who choose to live close to Him? We know that we feel more deeply towards that one of our children who draws closer to us than the others.

Whether we're one of God's little children or His big children, if we love Him we are special to Him.

Perhaps it brings a warm smile to our Saviour, nevertheless, when one of His own asks, "Lord, do You love me as much as ————?"

We have the evidence of His love all around us. We read it in His Word; we feel it in our heart; we know it in our mind. The hymn writer speaks of it as being "Loved with everlasting love."

And it makes us feel very special.

30

The Plus of Appreciation

Jean Anderson stepped into the living room just as her preschool Judy was saying to her little friend, ". . . all right if you 'preciate it."

Judy turned to her mother. "Mom! What does *'preciate* mean?"

Then, with a childish switch of attention, she skipped off with her friend to play outdoors before the mother could think how to explain the meaning of the word. But the question lingered. Jean couldn't imagine why her little girl had used the word, especially since to her it was only a series of syllables. *Appreciate. Just exactly how would I define it?* she asked herself. While she was still trying to decide, an almost forgotten incident came to her mind.

A few of the neighbors had been discussing their husbands' position and how far each one might go. One of the young women had made the statement: "I believe my husband will go just as far as I appreciate him into going."

She was a wise girl, this neighbor, for not only would her husband go far but her children would see in their mother a pattern that would likewise cause them to appreciate their father. Psychologists tell us that one of the finest things one parent can do for a child is to appreciate the other parent *and show it.*

The girl who grows up in an atmosphere where her mother appreciates her father will almost certainly have a right attitude toward her own husband. The same is true of the boy who grows up conscious that his dad appreciates his mother.

So back to the tot's question: "What is *'preciation?*"

It's respect. It's approval. It's acceptance and honor. It's saying, "I *knew* you could do it," in contrast to "How in the world did *you* ever manage to do that?" Importantly, appreciation is the antithesis of *de*preciation. If we were to keep score for a week or a month, I wonder how often depreciation would cancel out our expressions of appreciation?

This would be a good week to begin to major on showing appreciation. Automatically, any built-up habit of depreciating the members of our family would start to change.

Not only our husband but each of the children will go just as far as we appreciate him or her into going.

Maybe, thought Jean, *the best way to define 'preciate for Judy is to show her,* and she determined to do just that.

Out of the mouth of babes, she said to herself.

74

31

What a Silly Question

The leader of a professional seminar prefaced his remarks with "Remember! There is no such thing as a silly question."

I thought, *What a wonderful thing for mothers of small children to consider!*

Questions are here to stay and to be handled, whether we like them or not; and who among us has not been wearied at some time or other with the eternal *why, why, why?*

We have some alternatives when the children come at us with questions. We can turn them off with "What a silly question!" Or we can just listen; frequently the question itself is a bid for attention, as we all know. Or we can give as good an answer as we know.

It pays not to fudge. If we don't know the answer, there's nothing wrong with an honest "I don't know the answer to this one, son." The child will appreciate our honesty. And imagine—something Mom doesn't know!

Then we can go the next step and *learn with* the boy

or girl who poses the question. (Isn't that what all those wonderful encyclopedias are for?)

There's something warm and companionable about two heads in one book. Perhaps, in years to come when the particular item of knowledge comes into use, your son or daughter will remember the moment Mom took to search for an answer to the question.

We can be sure there will be numerous questions to which we have no answer, for surely we are living with the brightest generation of children who've ever lived. Then, too, some children are unusually intelligent, creative, and imaginative.

The response with which their questions are met at home will shape their thinking as to the worth of asking other adults for helpful information.

For example, if Mary has a mother who always turns her off and never makes an attempt to answer her questions, this girl will undoubtedly grow up with a "What's the use of asking? They never tell you anything" attitude; and it will include others besides her parents. How much she will miss all through the school years!

I'll always be grateful to the speaker who showed me that there are no silly questions.

32

Say Yes, Mom

Marilyn switched off the mixer so she could better hear her eager-eyed seven-year-old.

"Say yes, Mom," Ginny pleaded.

"Yes for what?" her mother asked.

"If you say I can do it, I'll tell you," bargained Ginny.

To her, this was a reasonable concession; but, as you or I would in a similar situation, Ginny's mom required a little more information before committing herself to say yes.

Her little girl's perfectly natural expectation was the basis of a lesson Marilyn long remembered. As she thought over Ginny's impulsive, almost demanding request that she give an unqualified assent to what the child wanted to do, this mother was reminded of an incident that had occurred some weeks earlier. Marilyn had gone to an older friend, a mature Christian in whom she had a great deal of faith and who had time to spend in prayer.

"I want you to pray with me," she had said, "for I have to make an important decision."

To her amazement, the friend had replied with the question, "Tell me, have you made up your mind and you want to ask me to ask God to bless what you've already decided to do? Or are you genuinely interested in God's guidance in this matter you're asking me to pray about?"

The searching question had caused Marilyn to face up honestly to the request for prayer as an aid in making her decision.

I guess maybe I was just like my own little girl. I wanted God to say yes to what I already had made up my mind to do, she said to herself, *instead of seeking God's will in the situation.*

That evening, as she spent time with her little daughter before putting her to bed, very simply she related her child's request to her, to our requesting things from God.

". . . so you see, dear, when we pray 'Thy will be done' we're saying to God that we want what God knows is best for us."

"Like I shouldn't say to God, 'Say yes and I'll tell you,'" Ginny elucidated, with the amazingly uncluttered wisdom a child at times exhibits. "Is that what you mean, Mommie?"

"That's right, honey. But not just you. Me, too," her mother assured her. "You see, grownups—mommies and daddies—should always say, 'Thy will be done,' when we ask God for something."

Stifling a sleepy yawn the little girl snuggled under the bed covers. "I'll remember," she half muttered.

Her mother's "amen" was a softly uttered, "Me too, Lord."

33

His and Hers

In the manner of children in most homes, Janice was standing in the doorway of the bathroom, watching her mother give some final touches to her hairdo.

With a quizzical look, Janice said, "Mom, why do just you and Daddy have towels that say 'His' and 'Hers'; why don't Jimmie 'n me have that on ours too?"

Without a doubt, Janice was speaking only for herself in the realm of towels. Her brother was too normal a boy to be even mildly interested in towels or soap and water or anything connected with "clean" at his age.

Do you suppose the young girl was really asking a question that had deeper implications than her question indicated? Was she, perhaps, making a plea for privacy, for ownership of some items all to herself?

Sometimes, in our desire to instill the virtue of *sharing in a child* (and this is good), we overlook the need for him to have some things of which he can say, "This belongs to me."

I know some mothers who extend the "joint ownership" concept even to their children's birthdays. A friend or relative who gives a present to the birthday child is expected to provide one for the brother and sister also. This idea may have merit which has not yet occurred to me, but the disadvantages seem pretty obvious. The special day belongs to the one who is celebrating his birthday, and others in the family should share the joy without having to share by receiving gifts.

Another "His" and "Hers" that a child needs is a *place* of his own. Conditions don't always allow for a separate room; but some special area can be arranged: a set of shelves, a closet, perhaps, that belongs exclusively to one child in the family.

Without this place of his own and belonging of his own, a child finds it difficult to respect other people's property. For instance, it's futile to say to a child who doesn't quite know what is his and isn't, "Now give Johnny back his bike (or whatever). You know you have your own."

Certainly we want to teach our children to share whatever they have. But how much better that this should be a voluntary gesture on their own part. It would be interesting to find out, for instance, if the little grabbers, the "mine-mine-mine!" kids, ever are taught at home the combined pride of ownership and respect for the other child's property.

Just one more aspect of "training *up* a child."

34

Dealing with Honest Doubt

Maybe it was his name, Tommy. Certainly his mom could scarcely recall a time in his life when he had not questioned just about everything. His speech abounded with "Why," "How do we know," and "Can you prove it?"

"An inquiring mind," the school principal called it; and he appeared to think it commendable. But then he didn't have to live with this young "doubting Thomas."

Have you, perhaps, had the same problem and found it disconcerting?

Maybe we should think about it for a few minutes.

Is doubting an evil thing or are we ready to concede that there may indeed be a good measure of faith in honest doubt? It takes courage to be able to stand out from the crowd and say, "I would really like to believe, but I'm just not sure."

Thomas, the disciple, must have been this kind of person. What a lesson we can learn from his doubting and Christ's handling of it. If the Scriptures teach us anything at all on the subject of honest doubt, it is that the Lord Jesus recognized Thomas's dilemma in believing. Our Lord's response to him is completely different from His reaction when the Pharisees and others voiced their skepticism to Him.

What if our Lord had been outraged at Thomas's avowed unwillingness to believe that He was alive, without the evidence of his senses! Suppose Christ had disowned him: "You're no disciple of mine!" But, no. Jesus understood Thomas and provided what he needed for belief; and the result was genuine, unreserved worship: "My Lord and my God." All doubt was dissolved (though ever since Thomas has been beaten over the head for his honest doubt).

Our children may come to the questioning stage, possibly doubting if they have a faith of their own or if it is a "faith of their father's." Rather than squelch the utterance of honest doubt, we should rejoice in the faith whose gropings spark the doubt, and help our boy or girl to get a fresh glimpse of the Saviour. He will stand the test; He will not turn His back on the young seeker.

Perhaps you can think of some issue—spiritual or moral—that was never really settled for you until you could figuratively take it out and look at it honestly. Doubt? Yes, but it is the desire to believe that gives us the courage to admit to having doubt.

So don't give up on the doubter in your family, even if his name *is* Tommy.

35

To Give and to Forgive

Allan and his sister Terry had been arguing for some minutes before their mother felt it was time for her to step in.

She attempted to listen as both children gave their high-pitched explanation at once. Through it all came the phrase, "But I won't forgive you!"

It was the common enough scene where little sister tinkers with her older brother's prized hobby and upset things. Terry had raised Allan's ire, and he had screamed at her. She had retaliated in little girl fashion and resorted to tears. That's when mother came into the picture.

Aware that he had hurt his sister's feelings, Allan compensated by offering her one of his miniature cars "for keeps," but, to nail down his disapproval of her action, he added, "You can have this—but don't think that means I've forgiven you."

Giving—but not forgiving.

Is this an exclusively childish trait, or does honesty

make us confess to harboring some of the same feelings at times?

It is easier to give than to forgive, of course. Generally, giving doesn't touch our inner life, doesn't make us face ourselves to the degree that forgiving does. But what of the relative consequences? For example, small Terry can hold in her hand the toy given her by her brother, but in possessing the toy she can't enjoy his goodwill. Fortunately, in the case of children, these feelings may (and they may not) be short-lived.

Moving into the adult realm, "I won't forgive you," cuts with razor sharpness: deep, scarring. No gift from the unforgiving person can ever begin to compensate for this kind of hurt.

So, wouldn't we be helping our children build a marvelous character trait by teaching them early the lovely grace of forgiving?

Why is this so important? Is it so that children and adults too will enjoy fine interpersonal relationships throughout life? Yes, but this is just a by-product, a bonus. The primary reason for majoring on having a forgiving spirit is its eternal perspective:

> For if you forgive others their trespasses, your heavenly Father will forgive you, too; but if you do not forgive people, neither will your heavenly Father forgive your trespasses (Mt 6:14-15, *Berkeley*).

We will not have to wait until we get to heaven to enjoy the fruits of a forgiving spirit, however. We will have good relationships with other people now, and to this will be added the smile of God. We'll find that it pays to both give and forgive.

36

Sticks and Stones

Can you remember when you were young enough that when something hurt, you ran to your mother for comfort? Perhaps someone had hurt your feelings by calling you "sissy," "scaredy cat," "chicken," or some other name that had power to wound.

Did your mother or an older sister or brother try to salve your feelings with the words,

> Sticks and stones may break your bones,
> But names will never hurt you?

Of course the older person really meant well and undoubtedly believed the advice being given you. You listened, but the words held no comfort.

None of us is very old before he learns that names do indeed hurt. Actually, name-calling is much more destructive and has far longer effects than a body blow delivered by a pugnacious playmate.

One of the ways in which names carry the power to harm is when we hear them again and again. For example, call a child "stupid" each time he has a small mishap, and this may well become self-fulfilling. He will begin to see himself as stupid. This impression will be difficult to erase once it is firmly imprinted.

What mother would want to be guilty of damaging her child in this way?

Any child, given the choice, would rather take corporal punishment than a tongue-lashing any day. (Ask yourself what your preference would be in this matter.) Ask yourself why your boy or girl prefers almost any form of punishment to that of being "talked to"? All too often, mothers stoop to name-calling, and the sting lasts.

Another form of name-calling is so despicable that it should never be indulged in by a Christian. This is the malicious name-calling behind a person's back, closely akin to slander. James has much to say about the use of the tongue for this purpose, and none of it is good.

Are we surprised when one of the children comes out with a name against someone else? Maybe we should ask ourselves, "Where did my Tommy learn such a thing?"

It may be that we should reverse our thinking about this couplet our mothers recited to us. For, while a band-aid can make a cut feel better, and a bruise will disappear after a few days, the hurt that accompanies being called names will not be so quickly healed.

37

More Than a Game

"You mean you sit your kids down and make them learn Bible verses!"

The tone of the speaker indicated her complete incredulity. It was as though she had just listened to a tale of child torture.

"Yes, I do," admitted the mother to her visitor, qualifying her assertion with, "Well, not quite 'sit them down' as you put it. In our family we have a practice of saying to each other the new Bible verses we have learned. It gets to be a kind of game. But, believe me," she added, "it's much more than a game. The verses I've learned have kept me close to God through the years."

This mother has pinpointed one of the deplorable failures of many Christian homes: the neglect of the Bible itself. How often at family worship (and this, too, is becoming something of a rarity in our helter-skelter lives) something else is used rather than the Bible. As the author of a number of daily devotion books,* I should be the last one to suggest a curtailment

Designed For Duty, Daily Assignment, Salt in My Kitchen.

of their use. Nevertheless, it's the Word of God that is living and powerful. Our best "thought for the day" comes from the Scriptures.

How potent is the Bible as a developer of values? For example, the editor of a New England newspaper, short of copy for his editorial page one week, printed the Ten Commandments in their entirety and without comment. A few days after publication he received a letter that said, "Cancel my subscription. Your paper is getting far too personal." And a farmer (exasperated with having his orchard rifled and finding his No Trespassing signs ignored, posted "Thou shalt not steal." That stopped the thievery.

We can teach our children many worthwhile things. Nothing, however, will have the deep, lasting, personal influence on them that the Scriptures will have throughout their life. Even if we do have to "sit them down" and encourage them to learn.

There's much to be said for the game method of familiarizing a family with the Bible. Alphabet games (*A* for Abraham, and on through *Z* for Zephaniah) can be used also with countries, rivers, etc. Twenty questions brings to light obscure objects and incidents in the Scriptures. It's fun, too, to piece together a psalm, the Beatitudes, or a favorite chapter or portion of the Bible.

What better way to use travel time, for instance? The miles slip by; and, unwearied, the children, with minds like sponges, soak up and store precious knowledge.

38

Puncturing the Gloom Balloon

Anne approached her almost-new neighbor a little hesitantly. After all, you don't pressure a person right at the first, and Marie had been gracious about accepting Anne's initial invitation to join her and her family in church.

"Oh, well, she can just say no," Anne rationalized and went ahead with her second invitation.

To Anne's delight Marie expressed interest in going again the following Sunday. Some weeks later as the conversation turned to churchgoing in general, Marie confided, "Know what first captivated me about your church? The positive way your minister begins the service with 'This is the day the Lord has made; we will be glad and rejoice in it.' He has a way of saying it as though just in saying and believing it something good must happen that day."

"Hmmm! I never thought of it like that, Marie, but you surely have something there," Anne agreed. "Now that you bring it to my attention, I can just see Pastor. It's as though he's making an official proclamation."

"Exactly. That's what I mean," Marie chipped in. "Sort of like a guarantee a thing will happen. I've heard the same verse in other churches, but it didn't do anything to me. Maybe the minister saying it did not believe it *was* the day the Lord had made or that God was in charge of it."

It was an intriguing thought and Anne couldn't get it out of her mind. She talked it over with her husband that same evening, and a determination was born. Together they agreed to experiment with this new insight at the breakfast table the next morning.

Family devotions began with the pronouncement, "This is the day which the Lord hath made; we will rejoice and be glad in it" (Ps 118:24). Each morning a different member of the family took a turn at being the announcer.

"You know, Mom, I'm beginning to believe this. Lots of times through the day it seems I keep remembering it, too," said the thoughtful junior high miss.

"Me, too," nodded her sophomore brother." It's kinda like puncturing the gloom balloon or something."

Who can predict the good effect on a family of starting out the day with a positive pronouncement from God's Word? What will it mean in the years ahead for this boy and girl as they develop positive spiritual attitudes that stem from knowing the God who not only made the day but who is in charge of it, as the insightful neighbor detected and expressed?

And daily, in the meantime, each one is contributing toward "puncturing the gloom balloon."

Can't think of a better way to do it, can you?

39

I Make Them Nervous

Jean Olsen laid aside the women's magazine she had been reading, her thoughts still occupied with a suggestion in a "How To" article.

"One way to make sure where your own young people are is to have the WELCOME mat out for their friends," the writer submitted.

You can imagine how surprised Jean was when her suggestion that Rick call and invite a couple of his friends for dinner the following evening fell flat.

"Maybe some other time, Mom," he hedged. "Not today."

Pressed for an explanation (*after all,* the mother thought, *I'm doing what the experts recommend*) the ten-year-old hesitantly said, "You make them nervous, Mom. That's what the guys say." He scratched his head in embarrassment. "Yeah, they told me you make them nervous when they're around our house."

I make them nervous! Jean managed to veil her dismay, taking it out to look at later when she was alone.

Why do I affect the kids that way? she asked herself. *I had it figured the other way around. They make me nervous.*

Discussing the subject with her neighbors (mothers of the boys whom she made nervous) she found their thinking reflected her own.

"I never know how to take them," one mother admitted.

"If I just knew what these kids were thinking," another added.

"I steer clear of them with their music and their silly jokes," a third neighbor chipped in. "They surely make me nervous."

Mrs. Olsen listened and probed deeper into her own reactions to her son's friends.

How did she make them nervous? How could she remedy the situation so that they'll want to come to her home?

She began to check herself, to let out a minimum of "What *are* you doing?" with the tone that connoted, "Whatever it is, it has to be bad."

She began to listen at least as much as she talked, and a new kind of relationship began to develop between herself and her son. With a warm glow she acknowledged a new insight into Bible truths with which she had long been familiar.

"Love suffereth long and is kind," Paul wrote in what we have come to call the love chapter of the Bible (1 Co 13).

This is what love is all about—suffering (tolerating) without appearing to do so. And being kind.

It takes some doing, to be sure, and nothing makes this possible—nothing but practicing the presence of Christ, letting Him live His life in us.

When the love of Christ shed abroad in our hearts causes us to see our children *and their friends* as persons to whom we can exhibit this love, things begin to happen. We cannot explain how it happens; but subtly, certainly, they will begin to realize that we don't make them nervous anymore.

And because we don't make them nervous—you guessed it—they will not make us nervous either!

40

Who Needs Boundaries?

"Why should I make my little boy do something if he doesn't want to?"

The smartly dressed young mother asked her question with a certain amount of belligerence. She added, "He'll grow up soon enough and then everybody will be telling him what to do and how to do it. I want him to have a happy childhood."

Older mothers can be counted on to snicker (if they don't laugh out loud) at this young woman. Rather than simply pooh-pooh her philosophy, however, we should give it a little solemn thought, maybe ask ourselves some questions.

What, for instance, are some of the certain effects of this mother's permissiveness? On the child, I mean. There was a time when, according to many people, the total dire result of permitting a child to do what he wanted was that "the mother was making a stick for her own back."

Thinking of this small boy, though, what is his moth-

97

er programming into his life in the present and for the future? Is she guaranteeing him the happy childhood she envisions for him?

What are some of the things that make for happiness in a child? Boundaries, for one thing. The security of "thus far and no farther" tells the child intuitively, "Mother cares about me. She doesn't want me to get hurt."

Three and a half-year-old Billy realized this. His mother had no idea of allowing her boy to do what he wanted to do all the time, and she made this plain to him. His home was on a busy street, and he knew he could ride his tricycle only as far as the line that was drawn for him in the driveway. One day he appeared at the kitchen door with the request, "Mommie, will you please make a new line? I can't see the old one anymore."

Suppose his mother had shrugged this off with "Never mind, son. You can ride your bike wherever you want to." This would have come across to him as something akin to "Go play in the traffic" and would have been interpreted as "Mommie doesn't care what happens to me."

Besides robbing a child of security, permissiveness is unfair in other ways. Frequently such a boy or girl, brought up without boundaries, is obnoxious to other people. If the mother who has so disadvantaged her child could assure him that she would always be there to tolerate his actions, it would be bad enough. But often an undisciplined child or young person is cast adrift in a world that will not put up with his attitudes and actions. All too often, emotional problems develop, some of which are never resolved throughout the person's life.

True mother love gives the Bible a place in the upbringing of a child, training him *up* in the way he should (not would) go. This is God's formula for a happy childhood.

41

Situation Ethics in the Home

Can you recall times when you were growing up when you couldn't make out head or tail of your parents' actions? You did something which they disapproved, and they reacted as you expected they would: punishment in one form or another. Then a week or so later you forgot the consequences and repeated the offence. But this time—no punishment! Of course you didn't push the matter, but you did wonder.

No one was talking situation ethics yet, but the practice was prevalent in some homes nevertheless.

Nancy Smith was reminded of this inconsistency in her own childhood when one day she heard a young relative talking to her son, Tim.

"I know Mom and Dad were sore last time I did it (whatever the "it" was, Nancy was left to imagine), but you know parents. One time they punish you for something and the next time they let you get away with it. I don't know how they figure it. I guess it depends

100

on how they're feeling at the time. If something's bugging them, they take it out on us."

Such insight should be a solemn warning to us. How important it is that we be consistent. And what happens when we are not?

Naturally we can scarcely expect a normal child to appreciate punishment; but he's sharp enough to know that if an offence deserves punishment one time, it is equally punishable the next time and the next and the next.

Inconsistency tends to breed confusion in a child's thinking and leads to his developing mixed values and uncertain standards of right and wrong. Predictably he will grow up rationalizing about sin, telling himself a thing is right or wrong according to how he feels at the time or what the surrounding circumstances are when he does something.

Titus has a word for us along this line. He speaks of "this present world" (2:12), exhorting us to be godly *now*. This should say to us that what was godly, *is* godly and always will be godly. There is a consistency about godliness. It doesn't change with the times in which we live or the circumstances in which we find ourselves; it makes no allowance for situation ethics.

If we could read our children's and teenagers' minds, we might be able to untangle some knots of understanding. Among these we would find the confusion we have unwittingly helped to create by our own inconsistencies.

42

Not Now—Afterward

Two of the most commonly asked questions in a normal household are, "Mom, why can't I have it now?" and "Why do you always say *afterward?*"

Think back to when you were the age of your child. Was not one of the insufferable frustrations having your mother or father say, "Not now—after a while"? It was small comfort when they added, "You're too young."

If we are honest with ourselves, we will admit that the last thing we accept graciously is this *afterward*. We are no more reasonable than our children in this respect. But would it be good for us to live with no unfulfilled dreams or desires?

Because we are wiser and more experienced than our youngsters, we can bear to disappoint them. It's for the child's own good, however much it may displease him. Then how do we relate this to our own attitude toward our heavenly Father, the Source of all wisdom? How often as we have prayed—almost demanded, perhaps— the response has been, "Not now—afterward."

The realization of how we react to the discipline of delay should go a long way in making us empathize with our children in their frustration. We can help them to accept this as a fact of life more easily if they understand that Mom and Dad have to cope with the same feelings when an answer is not immediately forthcoming.

What a challenge it is for every mother to make the seeming denial and delay merely a part of God's individualized plan for each of His children! Happy are the children who understand this early in life and grow up in this secure belief. They will be spared much irritation of spirit. They will be able to tolerate what irks many, both young person and adult, until they come to the place of accepting: "Just now you do not understand what I do, but you will know later on" (Jn 13:7, *Berkeley*).

Not now—but afterward.

43

The Cure for Blackmail

It's a paradox of today's home life that many mothers who were reared with a healthy respect for their parents are apparently intimidated by their own offspring. We see this every day in the little blackmailer in the supermarket, for instance, loudly demanding, "I want this. Buy me this." And the mother capitulates.

What is she afraid of? More trouble from the toddler if she refuses his demands? Is she thinking about what people in the supermarket will think if she does what her common sense dictates she should do? More times than not, people near the scene shake their heads over the performance of both mother and child. We can imagine what these onlookers are thinking. This, however, is relatively unimportant. The vital factor to be considered is what such permissiveness does to the child himself. Not only the immediate but also the long-range consequences of children's behavior are the responsibility of the mother.

Ouch! Have I pricked a nerve by my use of the

word "permissiveness"? Am I right in assuming that this whole area creates a measure of confusion in your mind? And are you pondering just what is the right way? In all the barrage of voices, each purporting to stem from expertise, whose advice can we trust?

Have you considered how uniquely equipped we Christian mothers are for the business of bringing up children? We have faith in Christ and a knowledge of God's Word, and in His Word God gives specific, changeless instructions.

"How," you may be asking, "does this differ from what pediatricians, psychologists, and educators offer in their advice and instructions?"

Here is how it differs. The experts propagate their teaching in good faith, but they stop there. The plus factor in choosing God as our final child-training authority is that He enables us to follow through. Take, for example, the exhortation in Ephesians 6:4, "Provoke not your children to wrath."

"But *they* provoke *me*" is an understandably justified retort. However, the Christian mother has recourse to a fund of grace to meet such occasions. The One who gives the instruction gives with it the power to implement it.

After all, whose "well done" are we ultimately striving for in bringing up our sons and daughters? Christian child training calls for looking *up,* not for looking *around* to see how other people react to the way we bring up our children.

44

The Mother in the Mirror

It was nearing Mother's Day; and, in the manner of elementary school teachers, Ken's teacher had assigned a brief composition entitled "My Mother" to her pupils.

The papers were taken home, and Ken's mother shared hers with me. Ken had written: "My mother is about six feet tall. My mother is almost always happy. My mother smiles a lot."

She's not anywhere near six feet tall—except in the eyes of her son!

"She's nearly always happy." What a favored child, we will agree, to have a happy mother.

"She smiles a lot."

Have you noticed that this boy made no reference to what his mother *gives* him—just what she herself is?

The "smile" part of his letter interests me, for I've heard psychologists say, "A smile says to a child, 'Everything is all right between us.'"

Care to try an experiment? Stand in front of a mirror wearing your usual facial expression. Be honest!

Next, turn up the corners of your mouth and smile. There, you even feel better, don't you? Now ask yourself which face you would prefer to look at much of the day. I can't think of a better reason for having mirrors around the house, can you?

Some people say that Jesus never smiled. I can't accept that. Would little children have crowded around an unsmiling Saviour?

Smiling is far more contagious than gloom. First thing we know, we will have initiated a "brighten the corner where you are" campaign; and the whole family will join in.

Whether or not we can give our children all the material things we would like to give them, one thing is sure. A happy child comes from a happy home—rich or poor. In this one boy's mind, happiness is closely associated with a smiling mother.

Let's look in the mirror often until smiling becomes a firmly fixed habit. We might all end up "six feet tall!"

45

Think Good

What do I mean by "think good" you may be asking. I mean having the kind of thought reflexes that turn your mind to the possibility for good in a situation rather than immediately fearing the worst.

We all know such people. We can visualize some of the scenes in their homes. A telegram arrives, and with fluttering heart and shaking hands the person hesitantly opens it. Those who are close to this woman would never dream of sending a congratulatory telegram to her, whatever the occasion. They know it would have an initially adverse effect, for, to her, a telegram means just one thing: trouble.

Others "think bad" whenever a message is received concerning the health of a loved one. He's sick—then he must be dying.

"As a man thinketh in his heart, so is he" is more than a memory verse to learn: it is solid, practical fact. The person who sees calamity potential in every untoward happening is exhibiting what he is in his heart: apprehensive, fearful.

What happens to such a person each time his mind turns to dire inevitables? Anxiety takes over and, whatever his usual capabilities, he is less able to cope with the situation than if he were to face it unhandicapped by fearfulness.

I wonder, do we realize how our spirit of optimism or pessimism communicates itself to our children? What is more pathetic than the boy or girl who is emotionally crippled by the expectation of something bad happening? These children are old before their time, for mostly our image of childhood is of sunny, good days.

In particular, Christian mothers have a responsibility before God not to be unduly pessimistic. "Our times are in His hands," are they not?

Certainly there will be rainy as well as sunny days, but for the rain and the clouds God has promised the rainbow of His presence. What a joy it is to be able by God's grace to portray Him as He is: the One who knows all about what each day will bring and whose promise is, "As thy days, so shall thy strength be" (Deu 33:25).

Then, far from facing things with apprehension, our children will follow our example of trusting Him, of believing that, whatever the circumstance, the Lord will work *in the circumstance* for our good.

Let's think good, shall we?

46

But the Action Is Missing

The light that shines the farthest, shines the brightest at home. So goes the adage.

"Let your light so shine before men," Jesus said.

Before men. It may be that for many of us this includes men in the making. Little men. And the years will tell how clearly the light shone at home.

It was Youth Sunday, and the speaker—no radical, no hippie—a clean-cut university student, voiced the thinking of much of his generation.

"What disturbs us," he explained in a nonemotional tone, "is that, while the words are all in place and you *say* the right things, the action is missing. We don't want just to hear that you have peace. We want to be able to observe it. We need the security of seeing you older Christians living for God, proving to us that what you say you believe really works for you."

What a tribute he then paid his own parents as he

declared, "I've been fortunate. I've seen this consistency in my home all my life."

Part of "all his life" had been a stint in Vietnam, and he shared the secret of his having been able to maintain a strong witness for Christ while he was there.

"Spending time with God, reading the Word, and talking to Him in prayer had been instilled in me from early childhood. So, realizing I needed time to be quiet with God, I volunteered for the duty nobody wanted, the midnight to 3:00 A.M. guard duty. In the solitude I could commune with God and feel Him strengthening me."

Many a mother would give everything in the world as her boy goes off into the service of his country, to know he has this kind of bulwark for his faith and that she has helped to develop it in him.

Why do so many of us fail at this crucial point?

A mother highly respected in Christian circles tells with infinite sadness, "My married daughter asked me one day, 'Mother, why did we not have regular family devotions when I was growing up? I can't remember that we set aside a time each day for worship, to pray together as a family.' "

It's too late for this mother. Her children are grown and in homes of their own. But let her speak to you whose children are still with you, "I would urge you to *let everything else have second place.* Please don't ever have to hear your son or your daughter rebuke you with the question my girl asked me."

111

"Let your light so shine" the Lord Jesus still challenges us (Mt 5:16).

Let us determine that we'll not be guilty of having all the words in place but the action missing.

47

What's Wrong with Tears?

A shrill cry sent Marie dashing out the front door.

Four-year-old Jerry was gingerly picking himself up after a fall off his tricycle onto the sidewalk. Blood trickled from his knee, and grime from his little hands mingled with the tears streaking his face.

A neighbor joined them just as his mother coaxed, "Now don't cry, son. A big boy like you doesn't cry."

Her urging didn't stop the child's tears, however, as he stooped to grab his knee where it hurt. He sniffed a few times as his mother shushed him. "Just stop crying and we'll have it fixed up in no time," she insisted.

The neighbor brought up the subject later that day. "Why is it so important to you that Jerry doesn't cry?" she inquired. "Are you trying to prove something or what?"

"Whatever makes you think such a thing?" Marie defended herself indignantly. "Of course I'm not 'trying to prove something,' as you put it. It's just that—" She stopped, at a loss to explain even to herself.

It could be that this young mother had grown up in a family where it was considered weak or childish to cry. She was most likely hushed every time she cried, with a reason or without; and she was just continuing the pattern. Now that it was brought to her attention, she could recall times as a little girl when something hurt and she was never permitted to cry. Consequently, she had grown up unsympathetic, cold even to her four-year-old.

Do we, as Christians, sometimes place undue emphasis on stoicism, on taking things well. Do we forget that our Lord wept openly at the grave of Lazarus so that onlookers commented, "Behold how He loved him!"

And what about the verse in Ecclesiastes that there is "a time to weep" (3:4)?

Who will dispute that the child who is allowed to express his hurt in tears will grow up to be much more sympathetic and understanding of other people's sorrow than the one whose feelings are constantly squelched with "Big boys like you don't cry"? He gets the impression that tears are "sissy."

These deep feelings, internalized, may surface later on in some form of emotional maladjustment.

Janey had a more balanced childhood. She related to her mother one day, "Mommie, my friend's little kitten died and I showed her I was sorry."

"How did you show her, dear?" her mother asked.

"I *cried with her*," Janey said.

Her tears had not been arbitrarily condemned, and

she was able to find a sure means of showing that she cared when another person was hurt.

It's my guess that she knows how to rejoice with those who rejoice, as well as to cry with those who cry.

48

Removing the Sting

How often the question is raised, "How do I tell a child about death?"

One good answer to this question comes under the heading "making devotions relevant."

The Adams family had read as their scripture at devotions I Corinthians 15:53-58. They read in turn; and when they had finished, Billy asked, "What does it mean about stings. Is it like when a bee stings you?"

Billy's mother looked at his dad, the kind of look that says, "Go on. You tell him."

After a brief explanation, the father encouraged his wife to continue with a story Billy could comprehend.

"Your daddy," she began, "knew I was awfully scared of bees. He liked to have some fun; and one day he caught a bee, tied a thin string around it and let it go. It came in my direction and I screamed. Not till then did Daddy tell me that the bee's sting had been removed, that it had already stung somebody, and now it had no power left to sting."

Around the table that day the Adams family discussed the fact that Jesus had died to take the sting out of death and that it could never sting us, if we accept what Jesus did for us. They talked about dying as just going away from each other for a while and going to be with Jesus, then one day He would come again and there would be no more death.

Not long after this discussion, Billy's grandfather died. They had been great pals, until the time a few months back when Grandpa had fallen and broken his leg. After that, Grandpa had spent most of the time in a wheelchair.

When Mrs. Adams told her young son about his grandfather's death, Billy was quiet for a few minutes. Then, with a bright smile, he said, "Wasn't it *nice* of Jesus to come and take Grandpa to His house? Grandpa won't need his wheelchair anymore."

At any age, what a comfort to know that the sting has been taken out of death. No child should have to live with unanswered questions until a member of the family goes to be with the Lord. At such a time he is often left to wonder, while the adults care for what has to be done at the time of death.

Children should be prepared while death is still not a reality to them, for it can be a traumatic, scarring experience. Fortunate is the child who has an acceptable introduction to death, the most predictable fact of life.

49

A Hand on Mine

The scene is as common as the combined presence of
an adult, a child, and a lawnmower. We've all observed
the small boy or girl who, having watched with interest
an adult mowing the lawn, approaches with the com-
mand, "Let *me*."

Impatiently the little dictator pushes aside the strong
adult hands. You can visualize the next part—vain
struggling by the child, unwilling to admit defeat. After
a few tries he reluctantly gives up. At this point, Daddy
or Grandpa or whoever is doing the grass-cutting, gently
places his hands on the small hands. Together they re-
sume the mowing. But who is doing the work!

Isn't this just like us? We like to think we can go it
alone. We struggle in a near futile effort at complete
independence, not really getting very far.

Our Lord's words, "Without me you can do nothing"
(Jn 15:5) is a hard saying. We could accept "Without
me you won't accomplish quite as much": but *nothing?*

Like our own children we frequently have to come to

the end of our own ability before we feel, suddenly, that gracious hand on ours.

> There is grace and power in the trying hour,
> In the touch of His hand on mine.

Why do we resist so long? Ultimately we swing to the conviction that "I can do all things through Christ who strengthens me" (Phil 4:13), rather than childishly insisting "*I* can do it. Let me."

Independence dies hard, for it's bred into our very nature to try to get along without God. And the Lord lets us try, just as we allow our children the same privilege. All the while we're watching their struggling attempts to do something that's beyond their strength and ability, we are inwardly saying, "That should prove to him he can't manage alone"; and after a little while we offer our help.

While we place the helping hand on a child's, wouldn't this be an excellent opportunity to teach him the lesson of a lifetime: that he needs God's hand on his? How much frustration he will be spared through learning early that God's strength is made perfect (and demonstrated to other people) as we allow Him to help us in our weakness.

Knowing this, far from resisting and pushing away, we will reach for another hand on ours—God's hand.

50

Rights and Privileges

Martha was obviously out of sorts as she tossed her books on the kitchen table.

"I don't think much of our neighbor, Mom," she griped. "All we wanted to do was ride our bikes across that little corner of her lawn, and did she fuss at us. Wow!"

In this situation would you be likely to side with your girl or boy, or would you point out that the neighbor has rights which deserved to be respected?

One of the most basic lessons we can teach our children is that one person's rights end where they violate the rights of another.

A little child can't be expected to know that, while he would love to ride all over the neighbor's lawn, the neighbor has the right not to have his lawn mutilated by trike tires.

It's when we fail to teach this principle early that we raise little rebels who predictably become big rebels. Foot-stamping and demanding things as a right is natural for the young child. (Have you noticed that you never have to teach a child to do wrong?) When we consider where the traits come from and when we think how much trouble these arrogant attitudes have caused us, we'll want to spare our children the same kind of heartache. It's never too early to begin.

We all know young persons who have been robbed of this parental teaching. Allowed to ride roughshod over other people and their property as children, they continue the practice and have a rude awakening when other people don't let them get away with such actions.

How much better it is when we explain to the child that certain things are privileges, not rights; that when the Browns next door let him invade their property this should be regarded as a favor, a privilege, sometimes a very special privilege. A spirit of gratefulness will then be fostered instead of the obnoxious, take-it-for-granted "I have a right to it" attitude that characterizes many of today's young people and children.

We can begin with the three- and four-year-olds. We'll be doing them a lifetime favor by starting them out with a fine sense of the rights of others: for instance, the right of a playmate to take his toy home intact rather than broken by another child who felt he had a right to it.

51

Today Is the Day

Quoting a woman whose home had been threatened by a major fire in the Los Angeles area, a network newsman reported, "We're praying people. When it looked as though we might lose our home, we prayed. The Lord changed the direction of the wind and our home was saved."

Whether he was aware of it or not, this on-the-scene reporter intimated much more than the stated fact. We are given a glimpse into a family where faith can reach for a miracle.

Perhaps, as you have read of mothers in some bygone era, mothers whose faith resulted in miracles, you've felt a sense of deep longing for some of the same in your own family life. But maybe even your thinking along this line has been inhibited by "What would people think?"

Do miracles properly belong only to certain days, in the future, principally?

Martha in the Bible is an example of this kind of reasoning. She had a solid faith that guided her to do the accepted thing. When her brother became seriously ill, she knew what to do. She sent for Jesus.

You know the story. Days passed. Then Jesus assured Martha and her sister that their brother would live again.

Even in her grief, Martha's traditional faith came to her aid. Her words reveal the limit of her expectations. She believed in miracles, even to the extent of resurrection from the dead—but not *today*.

We will never stand in Martha's shoes. And we may never see our home threatened by fire. But, if we did!

Every day calls for a miracle of some kind. Do our children grow up knowing the exciting possibility of what God can and will do for them and for us now? Or is their concept of miracles that they are for "tomorrow"?

The mother who, through none of her own doing, finds herself in an impossible situation and calls on the miracle-working God is giving her children a lifetime object lesson.

Who can foresee what this generation of children will face as the days darken? We cannot protect them always. We can, however, through their daily awareness of the God of miracles, make Christ immediate to them, make prayer their ready personal resource. One experience will reinforce another as they live in an atmosphere of "what God had wrought" and "this is the Lord's doing."

Of course miracles are for tomorrow—and for today.

52

So They'll Come Back for More

Marge cast an "I give up" glance at her four-year-old Billy.

Her irritation with him showed in the way she jerked the clothes from her basket and stuck them on the line. Noticing Marge's manner, her neighbor Jane, also busy at her clothesline, asked, "Something eating you, Marge?"

"That kid!" Again she tossed a telling look in the direction of her son, happily racing his cars on the driveway. "I tell you, I'm at my wits' end trying to get him to eat. He gets worse all the time."

"Oh, I thought it was something real bad," her neighbor tried to mollify the frustrated Marge. "Getting a kid to eat is something we all go through. They grow out of it."

"Maybe yours did," Marge grudgingly admitted the possibility. Then, brightening, she asked, "What worked for you? I'm ready to try anything."

It was no new solution, no magic formula, that Jane

had to offer; but Marge did try and she did have a measure of success.

Undoubtedly, most mothers are aware of both the problem and the particular answer Jane shared: stop loading a child's plate. Give him a little at a time and make it look attractive. He'll come back for more.

The real value of this incident was that it set both women thinking of the spiritual analogy. Christian women, they had been diligently striving to win some of the other mothers whose children were their own children's playmates.

"We've been trying to stuff the gospel down their throats," Marge and Jane admitted to each other, with too many tracts and such."

They resorted to the "little-at-a-time, make-it-attractive, and-they'll-come-back-for-more" strategy; and gradually, in the way Billy began to show an interest in meals, the unsaved young women began to exhibit a glimmer of interest in the Bread of life.

Can we learn from this simple illustration?

How often has a mother's heart been torn as she has listened to a teenager or older son or daughter say with bitterness, "I might have been interested if they (Mother and Dad, usually) hadn't pushed the Bible and church and God down my throat."

Of course, 90 percent of the time this is not a valid criticism. We know this, but it is small consolation when we see someone we love drift ever farther from the Lord.

125

Maybe we need to begin to offer small, tempting bites. These will differ with different people: perhaps just the right book (there was never such a day of wide selection), perhaps inviting certain young people into the home. We may have to give up a particular church in order to take our children where "the diet" is more geared to their appetite than to ours. Certainly, becoming angry and frustrated at the noninterested boy or girl is no answer.

With honest intent and a genuine desire to see our children live for God, let's pray for wisdom to make our own faith so attractive to them that they will taste and come back for more.

Moody Press, a ministry of the Moody Bible Institute, is designed for education, evangelization and edification. If we may assist you in knowing more about Christ and the Christian life, please write us without obligation to:
Moody Press, c/o MLM, Chicago, Illinois 60610.